Child of God

You are already perfect — God doesn't make mistakes...

Learn to be your beautiful inner child,

all the time, inside and out

by Isak Griffiths

Isak Griffiths

Champaign, Illinois

2020

Cataloging-in-Publication Data (CIP)

Griffiths, Isak, 1968–
Title : *Child of God: You are already perfect — God doesn't make mistakes...*
Learn to be your beautiful inner child, all the time, inside and out / Isak Griffiths
p.   cm.

ISBN 978-1-951262-01-3 (Hardcover edition)
ISBN 978-1-951262-02-0 (Paperback edition)
ISBN 978-1-951262-03-7 (eBook edition)
ISBN 978-1-951262-04-4 (Audiobook edition)

Library of Congress Control Number: 2020901677

1. Self-actualization (Psychology). 2. Perspective (Philosophy).
3. Self-realization. 4. Happiness. 5. Self-help. I. Title.

DCC 158—dc23

Series: Zero to Faith, Book One.
ISBN 978-1-951262-00-6 (Zero to Faith)

Printed and bound on demand in the United States of America
First hardcover printing, 2020
First paperback printing, 2020

Visit www.HonestImpact.com

Dedication

Dear God,

From the little kid in me
to all that is glorious in You...

Thank you

Contents

Introduction

Nearly from the moment of my birth I felt like a colossal failure in every fiber of my being. I spent my early years surrounded by constant reminders that children like me were never supposed to be born. I had the constant sense that I had failed the purpose of my existence, or often that I didn't deserve a purpose at all — and I believed to my core that something was inherently wrong with me. I often lived with the sinking dread that I was deeply evil. It felt like the fact that I existed – that my mere existence – was... wrong. I spent the first almost-30 years of my life not being anyone in particular, and often not being anybody at all.

This book is my beginning. This is what I had to learn before I could begin to have an identity, to have a life, or to have a faith. It took me seven years to begin to believe that I was a child of love. If you are looking for a beginning, maybe this can be your beginning, too.

So this is not a book about me, and it is not full of memories or stories or anecdotes. It is a book about you. It is a book about you and what is true for you, whether or not you are ready to choose to be more. But... if you are ready to begin to believe – regardless of how you entered the world – I am here to tell you that you were sent here in Love. In beauty. And... in Faith.

God willing, my story will have a life of its own later on. But for now, you are the center of a universe of one. You are Perfect. And you are Loved.

I am not a doctor, a psychologist, or a psychiatrist. I'm not a healer, a shaman, or anything else along these lines. I am simply someone who has struggled deeply to understand why I have felt so broken, and why traditional and clinical strategies have often left me feeling even more isolated or more fractured than before. Quite simply, I think the "experts" have got it all wrong.

When I chose faith as a part of my life, I found that having faith – or more specifically *choosing* faith – helped in spits and spurts (and sometimes in great leaps). But it still felt like something significant was missing. Intuitively I understood that this something was a solution that only I could find because that solution was somewhere deep inside me.

Over the years I have slowly found ways to re-unify parts of what I call "me." While much of my learning has been framed by spiritual teachers that I love and trust, much has also been an instinctive response to things in my life.

If you are finding that the counseling, the self-help books, the pastoral advice, and the random advice of friends and families all leave a hole in your heart, I hope that some of what I have learned can help you find peace and meaning for yourself.

If you find that some things resonate and some things do not, hold on to what is useful and let the rest fall gently away.

If right now more of you than not wants to believe that God does not exist, or that God exists but makes mistakes, that's okay. Sometimes the thought of no god at all can hurt less than the thought of a god you do not understand. If that's the case, however, put this book aside for now.

Between wanting not to have faith and choosing faith are times of wishing you could believe. Sometimes, the first step is wishing you could want to believe in something bigger than yourself.

When you find yourself wanting to want more, come back to this book. Keep reading or listening to it over and over when that part of you is hungry for more. Pick a line that sings to your heart and repeat it to yourself until you feel the words sinking into your heart. Come back whenever you experience a window of hopefulness and find another bit that speaks to you. Keep coming back until you're ready to choose to begin to heal.

If you are ready to find your beginning...

I

Give yourself permission to find your own way

We live in a world that glorifies gurus.

In part, I think this is human nature. Throughout history, there are men and women who have been sought for their insights and wisdom. I think we have a deep down need to live in truth, and when we cannot easily find our way, we seek people who have found the courage to speak their truths in the hope that they can help illumine our own paths.

But more than anything, I suspect we tend to fall prey to a combination of good marketing and of being pack animals. There is a mountain lion in all of us who will spend every last ounce of life and energy chasing a clear goal, yet be more than content to laze in the sun on a thick branch until we're so hungry that we grudgingly accept that we must move or starve. Then, when we smell the herd or hear the stampede, we can't help but follow the masses in the hope of snacking on the low-hanging fruit.

It's a special creature that makes it to the front of the pack without getting trampled. The problem is that when you do get to the front, you either find a shyster who will take every last penny you have and convince you that you're worth the investment, or you will find a real guru who gives you a litany of unsatisfying answers: Look to God. Look within. Serve others. Pray. Have faith. Meditate. Find your center. Let go and let God. Forgive those who hurt you. Forgive yourself. Manifest more peace in your life. Be more mindful. Use daily affirmations. And so on.

Please don't get me wrong. I believe there is genuine value in these kinds of suggestions. I agree with their messages and have embraced many of them in how I live my life. But none of these simple statements or practices ever helped me heal. They helped me feel better in the moment and to help better manage new problems. They just didn't help me become more whole.

If that is true for you as well...

What if...

What if... the reason the answers from the gurus around you feel wrong is because their answers are simply that: *their* answers?

What if... the reason you keep looking for a better answer is because a part of you already knows that a better answer exits?

What if... the guru you really need is in truth one of those parts of you that feels broken and abandoned?

What if... the reason you feel more broken over time is because the harder you hunt, the farther and farther away you get from the hurt and frightened guru inside you that already has the answers?

I think...

I think the answer is already inside you.

I think the answer is calling to you all the time. I think a part of you already knows it.

I am not a guru. And I won't pretend to be able to tell you where to find your answers.

But I can tell you exactly where I found mine. I can tell you how I found my inner guru.

And I can tell you how it helped me heal. I am not a guru. I am simply human.

If you are simply human, too, then maybe... just maybe... what helped me can help you, too.

2

What's wrong with the traditional view of "what's wrong with you"

I used to do Google searches periodically on the mass of hurt and confusion I was feeling inside. More often than not, I'd come across articles saying I needed to heal my Inner Child. Just in case this popular psychology is new to you, check it out yourself. If your experience is anything like mine, I suspect you will "learn" several things about what the powers-that-be call your Inner Child:

- It is in some way segmented or separate from the core of you,

- It is often responsible for you behaving uncontrollably and/or irrationally,

- It is in need of nurturing and healing to give you access to a sense of innocence and freedom, and

- It is in need of nurturing and healing so that you can more reliably act like an adult.

Some of the experts on the Inner Child also place each person's natural curiosity, creativity, innocence, joy, and sense of boundless freedom inside what they describe as a traumatized and fractured sub-personality. Yet they mostly agree that to access all of the inherently awesome human powers, the Inner Child must first be comforted, healed, held, nurtured, and so on; the experts agree that we cannot be whole and happy until our Inner Child is healthy and happy.

To me there are all kinds of things wrong with this traditional view of the Inner Child.

1. It says that a core part of you is not only separate from the rest of you, but also small, weak, scared, and powerless. It frames a core part of you as a victim of your life that needs to be fixed and protected. It is alienating. It is patronizing. And it makes healing your heart and your spirit even harder by treating the part of you that hurts and

the part of you that can heal as two distinct and separate parts of you.

2. It completely fails to identify the "you" that is supposed to heal "your" Inner Child. If your creativity, curiosity, happiness, sense of freedom, anger, frustration, and fear are all a part of "your" Inner Child, then who are "you"?

Are "you" the rational mind? If so, wouldn't having a separate and well-contained Inner Child be a good thing? After all, then you wouldn't need to be distracted by pesky things like memories, random emotions, or unnecessary questions.

Are "you" the spiritual being? If so, wouldn't having a separate and well-contained Inner Child be a good thing? You wouldn't need to deal with desires for physical affection or superficial entertainment, or worry about other such silly worldly distractions.

If "you" are not your Inner Child, your mind, or your spirit, then who on earth are you?

3. It fails to account for how you are supposed to teach skills that you supposedly need to heal in your Inner Child in order to leverage those skills as an adult. For example, if you need to nurture your Inner Child in order to allow yourself to be more gentle and kind to yourself and others, how are you supposed to learn how to be gentle and kind so that you can nurture your Inner Child? More specifically, how are you supposed to assure your Inner Child that it is loved and valued if you don't love and value yourself?

In other words, the traditional view of the Inner Child implies that being a child is a condition to be outgrown and overcome — and that your Inner Child needs to be fixed so that you can be a fully functional adult. Your Inner Child is supposed to be the cause of road rage, procrastination, emotional distance, unhealthy boundaries, being unable to share, rebelling against authority, and other social ills.

But except for bullies on a playground, this is not how children behave.

Children are the antithesis of this. Children are, by nature, loving, trusting, courageous, and resilient.

Yes, they can be unruly, bratty, pushy, mean, cruel, and more. But that's just part of being human. The world we live in can be unruly, bratty, pushy, mean, cruel, and more.

This is not the fault of anyone's Inner Child. Instead, I think this is very much the fault of every adult who isn't working at all times to make the world a better place. In other words, it's the fault of the *grownups* within us all.

I think... I think we tend to emotionally cut off our Inner Child, and then blame it for not being there.

Here's what I believe is closer to the truth.

3

The roots of the kid in you

In your mind, picture the coolest tree you have ever seen. The only condition is that the tree in your mind must be alive and have roots.

That tree – like you – started as a single seed. It may have started to blossom before it even sank into the ground; it may have taken months or years to take root. But in time, with water and light, it reached both into the ground and toward the sun.

Maybe your start in the world was unexpected; maybe it was planned for years. Maybe you were planned and desired; maybe your conception was wrapped in pain. But you... and I do mean you... were a perfect seed.

As you grew, parts of you sank deep. Your family history, your early years, and every experience created or grew roots. Some took hold, and some ran into rocks, some ran deep. As you continued to grow, there was a light that fed you. Maybe you never saw the light, but if the light had not been there, you would not have grown.

Parts of you reached toward that light, fed on that light, and even began to bloom. You tried on different features, habits, thoughts, feelings, people, and more. Like leaves they grew strong and dark, and over time many have fallen away. But sometimes new branches and new possibilities would start to grow. And you'd develop a whole new side of you, all the while growing deeper into the earth, and upward toward the light.

I believe – like that seed – every part of you that found strength that is still with you is a part of you. Every memory that took root and strengthened, every branch that reached out for something new, every leaf of hope and of fear, every strand of moss that grew in the shade, every berry and fruit and seed of possibility.

Like a tree, though, no one root or leaf or berry is permanent. You can prune and clean and strengthen and grow. You can shiver and drop most of your leaves and start over. You can even feel like you are split in two, and grow back together and become that much more magnificent. But everything you hold on to – while you hold onto it – you make a part of you.

However, there is something unique about your tree: It was there in your seed. It is there in your roots. It is there in your leaves. It is there in the fruit you bear. It is there in core of you that reaches deep into the earth and that reaches upward into the sky. It is there in the core of you that is full of life.

It is the part of you that is a Child of God. It is your life. Your essence. Your roots. Your growth. Your fruit. And even the parts of you that you choose to let go that feed the roots of others who cross your path.

All of it is you. All of it is perfect. All of it is beautiful.

Some say the Inner Child is your subconscious... the part of your tree below the ground that has dug into the dirt like desperate fingers that won't let go... the part of your tree in the dark, crawling with insects, or even starting to rot away. They treat this part of you like something that's holding you back.

Often the roots are compared to memories that get so deeply rooted that your Inner Child cannot reach up toward the light. Often the "you" is described as the trunk of the tree, or even the branches; but almost always the trauma of your childhood is relegated to the deepest, darkest, hardest to reach roots that haven't seen the light of day in a lifetime.

They treat this part of you like a child who is so afraid of the dark that it's unable to look under the bed. Instead of holding your hand while you to open the door and turn on all the lights and point 100 flashlights all around the bed like floodlights, they take all the old moldy blankets and build a manky fortress; their actions make the under-the-bed even bigger and darker and murkier and scarier than it was before. Then they blame the kid in you for feeling more fear. This doesn't make any sense to me.

When there are roots, those roots create a foundation upon which everything else rests and relies on for support. When the foundation of your house cracks, you either pay thousands of dollars to repair it, or risk those cracks growing up over time through the floors and the walls throughout your house. When the foundation of your tooth cracks, you may need to have a root canal, or you may even need to have the tooth removed. If you wear makeup, badly applied foundation means your face could wilt. And in business, when financial foundations fall, agencies generally have to close their doors.

In general, a problem with a foundation means a problem with the whole. And this notion is at the heart of the traditional view of the Inner Child. It claims that there is a problem with the foundational Inner Child; therefore, it concludes that a person who feels wounded can never become whole, healthy, or strong unless you can replace, repair, or remove the roots.

I agree that this would make total sense, but for one small but critical fact – the foundation of each and every person cannot be broken, cracked, or flawed because the foundation of each and every person is the image and likeness of God.

In my experience, perhaps somewhat oversimplified, people often believe one of three things about God:

- God does not exist
- God exists but makes mistakes

- God exists and does not make mistakes

Regardless, in some ways it seems to boil down to this: either you believe that there is someone or something that is awesome and powerful and good, and that someone or something loves you more than life itself. Or you don't.

And if you don't, please know at the very least that I love you. When you are ready to hear them, my words with be here with with you. And if it helps, for now I can hold the space of belief for you that when when you are ready to open your heart to God, He'll be there already waiting for you.

For now, I will say this:

- If laughing has ever brought tears to your eyes...
- If you have known a single moment of peace...
- If you have ever believed in your toes that there had to be a better way...
- If you have ever wished with all your might that you could believe in something...
- If you have ever believed that you could accomplish something no one else said was

possible...

- If you have ever created something with your own hands that filled you with pride...

If any one of these things is true, there is a part of you that already believes in the existence of something holy... there is a part of you that already believes in miracles... there is a part of you that believes in you.

Even more to the point, there is a part of you that can only believe this because that part of you already knows it to be true.

You may have started as a single seed, but it was a seed made in the image and likeness of God. You, at your core, are perfect.

The roots that stem from your heart of hearts are all roots of love, possibility, innovation, community, and faith. Just as God cannot be corrupted, what He has made in you has not been corrupted. You are perfect. You are beautiful. You are a Child of God.

If there is an Inner Child, it is not some broken, wounded, half-human animal that lives in fear of harm, abandonment, or abuse.

It is a kid, perfect and whole, who is filled with curiosity, wonder, and awe. It is, at the same time, a *kid*... it is not all-knowing, it is not all-powerful, and it sometimes needs help to grow and understand the world around it.

But just like every part of an oak tree is part of that singular oak tree, and every juniper is the juniper from its leafs through its roots, you are a Child of God, inside and out. That little kid is the part of you that keeps pressing you to believe that – no matter how hard things get – there is a divinity that pervades all of existence... there is a bigger-than-life Something-Good.

That little kid is the image and likeness of God within you, perfect, and timeless, and tireless. It is the image and likeness of God, full of love, affection, and forgiveness. It is the image and likeness of God, the embodiment of light, possibility, and creation. No one can take this away from you because in every way that matters it *is* you.

4

Then why do I feel so much pain?

Why do I feel so much pain?

Because there are an awful number of things and people in the world that are not you, do not care about you, do not see the presence of God in you, and do not appreciate who you really are. And, there are an awful number of things and people in the world that don't particularly care.

Because we are made in the image and likeness of God, we are wired to be hyperaware of the presence of God. Because God is everywhere and in all things at all times, we are wired to see God, feel God, and be in fellowship with God at all times in all that we see and experience.

Sometimes I wonder if that is part of the appeal of megachurches. Similar to being in the audience at a young child's recital, in the stadium of a professional sports team, or in the concert hall of a world-famous musician, actively worshiping with thousands who passionately want the same thing as you must enfold you with a sense of being part of something much, much, much larger.

While I believe you can feel the presence of the Holy when you walk into a place where people have prayed, I have never been inside a megachurch; if thousands of people are routinely and sincerely praying there, I imagine it feels like sinking into a warm pool that soothes and washes your aches away.

I have experienced something similar in a mission church. Being in a space where people pray all the time for you by name, and being surrounded by a God who hears your name over and over in prayer, can be overwhelmingly peaceful and sublime. For me, part of that feeling of majesty and infinite belonging comes from praying with millions around the world and billions across and outside of time and space.

Unfortunately, the rest of life often looks and feels like none of these experiences. Instead, we often face people we love seeing imperfections in us, jobs that care about what we produce and not who we are, near and far neighbors who see us either as resources for making their lives better or as obstacles in their way, mirrors that say who we are is how we look to others, mass media campaigns that consistently insist that we will never be good enough no matter what we do or what we have.

None of these are from God. Yes, they may be creations by other children of God, but these challenges are not from God. Therefore, they are not a part of you.

In some ways, this is simple. If something brings you closer to God, it is a part of you. A long talk with an old friend, a movie that awakens a quiet place in your heart, the meadow or brook that reminds you that the world can be beautifully gentle, the painting that takes your breath away, the sunset that completely captures you, a worship of God that fills you with a joyful longing for more... These things are of God. And, therefore, they are a part of you.

Everything else is dross, chaff, clutter, sludge, silt, and distraction. I once heard a bishop describe the world around us as a pigsty. And in a lot of ways, I agree. But I tend to think of it this way: We create;

we can't help it; God made us this way. So at all times we are creating things that bring us closer to God, or creating situations that make it easier to forget about the love, the acceptance, and the forgiveness of God.

When a driver cuts you off, you can choose to pray for him to arrive at his own destination safely, or choose to direct your own anger at him.

When your boss blames you for his own mistake, you can focus on how to ensure the right work gets done the right way, or you can respond in bitterness and spite; you can focus on creating a new and better job for yourself, or you can make your place of work less enjoyable for others.

When you find yourself procrastinating, you can pray for guidance and choose to take action, or you can continue to avoid, stew, and stall, making any future action that much harder.

Every time we – or anyone – create a situation that makes it harder to embrace the presence of God, it's like dropping muck and mire in our own wake. Sometimes we retrace our steps and have to slog through our own mess. But more often I think we tend to leave mounds of refuse in our wakes for others to clean up. And when we do keep slogging over the same murky grounds, we slowly churn the rubbish we leave behind into toxic waste.

Remember your favorite tree? Imagine that the tree is you – strong, deep, tall, and perfect, smothered in grit and slag and slop. The grime is seeping into the ground and smothering your roots, the waste is building up around the trunk, there is slime weighing down the branches, and gritty, dirty, sand scratching its way into each and every leaf.

On top of being smothered by the residue of the world's godless choices, the weight of the world is pressing in on you from every side, and the people who are doing this to you are also trying to snuff out every flicker of light that shines through the filth being piled on you.

We all know that a part of the refuse we're stuck in is our own creation, and we know deep down that we are connected with everyone and everything else in creation; so, we tend to feel completely responsible for every drop of filth that comes our way.

It hurts because the weight feels unbearable. It hurts because when no one else sees our light, we feel like it isn't there. It hurts because it's suffocating. It hurts because every time we open our eyes, the mud oozes in and burns. And it hurts because we know that some things are – at least in part – our own fault.

Also, if we are aware that we have been piling our own goop onto other people, we tend to believe their struggles are our own fault as well.

It hurts because we start to believe this misery is something we deserve.

It all hurts because, when we look at ourselves, we start to see only a cesspool, a heap of scrap, or a molten pile of junk. It hurts because it gets harder and harder to fully be the kid inside us under all the filth and the waste. And we start to believe that this toxic mess is our core self because in time that's all we can see.

If we're resilient, we have moments and experiences of hope and light and clarity. We have moments when we remember that this is not how things are supposed to be. But those moments of peace and love and inspiration get slippery and harder to hold.

Smothered in darkness, it hurts because it can feel like it's all we have left. It hurts because we feel burdened, and abandoned, and alone. It hurts because it's a struggle to see our own light, let alone the light of God.

5

Then why do bad things happen?

Bad things happen because we live in a pigsty. It's almost impossible to walk through any mile of wet, slippery mud filled with iron nails, thick weedy roots, and jagged stones without at some point falling flat on your face. Even if you pray without ceasing, hold nothing but love in your heart at all times, and somehow manage to always be helpful in ways that others appreciate, a gust of wind will eventually land you in the muck flat on your back. It is the price of living in a world with free will, and sometimes that price is high.

Life can feel like a lightning strike splitting us in two.

Life can feel like a raging forest fire burning away even the ashes of hope. Life can feel like a million axes all at once hewing away everything we have ever loved.

Life can be hard all the way down into the marrow of our bones.

That is the price of living in a world with humanity, and sometimes that price is high.

It doesn't help that our memories have voices of their own. We hold onto memories like nuggets of gold and diamond because they feel like they are a part of us. And with each leaf of personal history that we hold on to, it's one more voice that we hear reminding us of its joys or fears. And while joy has a much softer, richer, deeper, and more sonorous voice, anger and fear and abandonment have much bigger voices, and often shout louder than any sense of peace that might be vying for our attention. Even louder are the voices of shame and regret for things we ourselves have done. And the loudest voices are the memories of regret and shame for the things we failed to do or say.

That is the price of living in a world with ourselves, and sometimes that price is high.

Life is hard. Life is painful.

I do not believe that time heals all wounds. I do not believe that God only allows us to face problems that we can handle. I do not believe everything happens for a reason.

I believe life hurts so much sometimes because...well... that's... Life.

6

Truth and spiritual youth

I also believe that God is a God of truth. He understands that life brings real pain.

I don't believe God expects us to not feel the pain or to heroically hold on to the pain. I think He wants to sit with us in our agony, wrap us up with His love, hold us while we cry, and help us clear away all the things smothering our spirit so that His light becomes brighter and stronger and clearer than the pain. Instead of pretending that the pain will get smaller or go away completely, He wants to make hope and love so much bigger that the pain simply feels small and weak in comparison.

Whether you are 4, 48, or 88, what matters to God is that you are very much His Child. He created you. He loves you, inside and out. And He feels every ounce of your pain.

He understands that sometimes your life is bigger than your spirit. He understands that sometimes your emotions are bigger than your body. He understands that sometimes your hurt is bigger than your hope.

He also understands that those hurts and memories and agonies are not you. They may be part of your experience. But. They. Are. Not. You.

YOU are a Child of God. YOU are spirit and light. YOU are perfect. YOU are love.

The more willing you are to fully be the kid in you that God created, the more you sink into the presence of God that surrounds you.

God's love is a raging fire that over time can sear away all of the layers of slag the world has slung at you.

God's love is a flood of purifying rain that can over time wash away the stinging grit and the piercing edges of your memories that cut to the bone.

God's love is the cool and soothing ointment that lifts and washes away the impurities of the world that try to find a home inside you.

God's love is the breath of life and hope that wraps and warms you when the world says you are cold and alone, and that cools and refreshes you when the world says you deserve anything less than God.

God's love is the stillness and silence that raises you up into the light of the sun, and that gentles the messages that say you should more, less, or other than God declares you to be.

The tree you imagine you to be can be destroyed by wind or water or fire. But the tree of *your* life was made by God, and made in the image and likeness of God. The world cannot destroy what was made by God and what He says is good. Regardless of how it feels sometimes, the world cannot destroy you.

You are already perfect. The problem is not how to heal your "Inner Child" because it isn't broken. That part of you... that core of you... it isn't frightened or shy, it isn't hurt or scared, it isn't beaten or bruised, it isn't anything except amazing.

Think about it... when we talk about small children, how do we describe them?

- Fearless
- Strong
- Resilient
- Funny
- Creative
- They don't hold grudges
- They are easy redirected to focus on good things
- They make friends easily
- They instinctively know who they can trust
- They laugh out load and enjoy being inane
- They have no sense of vanity – they are who they are
- They get lost in the moment when they play
- They love freely and generously

That is who you are. That is what God created you to be. The rest is crud and clutter; the rest just gets in the way.

The things that are good for you and that are from God help bring out this kid in you. They help you feel free and loved. They help you see the beauty in others. They help you see the beauty in you.

When people talk about things that are "childish" – things like temper tantrums, flash anger, brattiness, bullying, and rudeness – they are using the wrong word. Yes, kids sometimes act this way, but mostly when they are being forced to grow up and don't want to. These are behaviors associated with deadlines, power struggles, juggling responsibilities, and not getting nearly enough sleep. These are behaviors that come from growing up, not from being a kid. Even the isms that plague society (sexism, racism, ageism, classism, and so on) are beliefs and behaviors that children have to mainly learn... from adults.

This is not who God created any of us to be. We are – and always will be – His Children.

7

Light, love, and the kid in you

A deep breath, and brief review of what we've discussed so far along with additional implications:

- We live in a pigsty of a world.
- We all get to chose what to do and how to act; living in a world with free will sometimes has a high price to pay.
- All that yucky, heavy, depressing stuff... it's not you; it's the world around you.
- We all leave trails of muck and sludge... try not to judge anyone too harshly for the crap you walk through – remember, someone else is tripping over what you have left behind.
- Being a grown-up is overrated; it tends to make us leave even more silt and slag in our wakes.
- Part of why God is with us all the time is to help us burn and wash away all that yuck whenever it's too much.

- You are a Child of God, made in the image and likeness of God.
- You were created to love, to create, and to celebrate.
- You are fully you from the tips of your leafs through the depths of your roots.
- God is already within and all around you; you don't have to find Him because He will never be anywhere else.
- Since God is a part of you, you are already connected to the world's greatest guru.
- You are perfect. You are beautiful. You are a Child of God. And no one can take these things away from you.

- We are love and light in every fiber of our being. We are made in the image and likeness of God.
- Your memories are not you ... they are only a part of you if you cling to them for dear life.
- The voices of your memories are not the root of you. When you are ready to let them go, they will fly away.
- The fear, the doubt, the anger, the pain that you feel is not you. It. Is. Not. You.

- You experience it, yes. It can feel like it's the heart of you. But it is not you.
- Anything that can be burned, washed, oiled, or blown away cannot truly be a part of you.
- You are a living and breathing tree of life.
- You are a Child of God – how cool is that?

8

Clearing the way to the kid in you

How do you clear away the clutter and fully embrace being the kid in you that God created you to be? It is simple but not always easy.

Each person is unique, and therefore each person has a unique relationship with God. The right path for you is yours and yours alone. In all likelihood, you will at times walk along with others; it may be two at a time, it may be 2,000. But much of the time, it will just be you and God. Warning, though... God is often not in a hurry. Sometimes He may give you the softest nudge; He may take you by the had and gently lead you; He may frog-march you directly toward a particular destination.

But in my experience, it's mostly like walking a labyrinth. It often feels like I've been in this same spot before, and I'm walking uselessly in circles, taking ten steps back, or wandering off the path completely. Sometimes I even feel like I've been blindfolded and kicked off a ship in the middle of an ocean. But as long as I keep walking and offer my heart to God over and over and over, I eventually realize that I've become much more like the kid in me than I used to be.

In the Chronicles of Narnia, Eustace Clarence Scrubb accidentally turns himself into a dragon. In this form he begins to understand how others see him, and each new revelation is more painful than the last. Eventually, he wants nothing more than to be a kid again, but he doesn't know how; so, Aslan helps him understand that he needs to peel off the dragon on the outside to find the boy inside. Eustace tries. Like a snake shedding its skin, Eustace peels off his dragon hide. Again, and again, and again. But each time, he looks down and can only see himself as the same thick, scaly dragon. Eventually Aslan Himself grabs ahold of Eustace and peels back the hide. To the boy it feels like Aslan has pierced him through the heart and peeled away his very skin.

Like Eustace, we can each get through the endless layers of our history the same way; we can peel it away layer by layer. Or, we can surrender to what feels like having our own flesh ripped away in chunks at a time. Both ways work; one takes a lot longer, and one hurts a whole heck of a lot more. There are probably as many ways to strip away the barriers to our hearts as there are people who want to feel free. Know, however, that it will often feel like an endless and fruitless battle. But it won't be; the tender-hearted kid is very much inside you and you can get there.

9

Clearing the way
— A fresh start

The overnight transformation of a person that is complete and enduring is possible, but it is something I have rarely witnessed.

Instead of having every single inch of the entire dragon hide ripped away all at once, more often it is pulled away in layers and chunks. At any point in time, that hurts a lot less than having the whole hide flayed off, but some of the skin regrows between chunkings. Sometimes it will feel like you've taken three steps forward, then six potholes, one landslide, and an elephant stampede. But, fortunately, how you feel doesn't always reflect reality. If you keep peeling, you will gain far more ground that you lose.

If you are ready, though, to jump in with your heart, mind, body, and spirit, and if you are ready to never again rest under the slag that will keep trying to press you down, there are immediate actions you can take. Each one works, though, only if you are ready to make the same decision and commitment every day for the rest of your life. You will likely stumble and fall over and over. But getting back up as quickly as you can with purpose and conviction will always matter more than falling down.

- **Baptism** (or other water-based rite of new beginnings). Ponder for a while the fact that the world we live in has been literally shaped by water; water has leveled mountains and smothered volcanoes, yet it also has an ability to heal and soothe that is unparalleled. There is nothing on Earth that water cannot reach or wash away over time, and that includes everything in your life that isn't really you. Baptism is about surrendering yourself completely to purification and forgiveness – not only to something bigger than you, but also to the smallest hidden nooks and crannies of your soul. Like God, water is more powerful and more purifying than your anger, your stubbornness, or your fear.

- **Holy fire**. The prayer of desolation and absolute confession. Honesty is hard, often because the truth genuinely hurts. But holding onto a truth you do not want to face only makes everything in your life harder to enjoy and yourself harder for you to love. If you do not like what you see in the mirror, what secrets are you holding on to? Find a way to let them out completely... yell at God at the top of your lungs, submit to confession, or cry yourself into a puddle of pudding. Do whatever it takes. If there is something you are unwilling to face, it is smothering the life out of you. Warning – it probably has jagged edges that will cut you from the inside out as you let it go; it may very well feel like you will burn alive from the pain. But if you weren't already feeling all of that pain and more somewhere inside you, it wouldn't be a secret in the first place. Let it go.

- **Choose to repent**. We all tend to believe lies of guilt and shame; we tend to believe the lie that we are less than perfect; we tend to believe the lie that our mistakes and moments of bad judgment will haunt us for all eternity.

We carry the weight of the world on our shoulders and in our hearts, and we believe the lie that we will forever be buried by the choices we have made. Granted, those choices have helped the world smother any sense of inner light, but even when it feels like the sludge piled on us is filled with piercing rocks and shattered glass, it is important to remember that the sludge *is not you*. At every single point in time, you can choose to leave more waste in your wake, or you can choose light and life. Repentance is about saying to yourself in all honestly and earnestness, "I wish I had made a different choice. If I could go back and change it, I would. But I cannot change the past. However, I *can* choose to leave that decision in the past and I *can* make sure I never do something like that again. I choose to be the Child of God that God created me to be. I chose love. I choose faith. I choose to make the world a better place. And I choose now to make this my choice again, and again, and again."

- **Choose to forgive others**. Nothing in this world that is part of the pigsty is a part of what it means to be human. Nearly every person in your life and that you encounter is buried under their own pile of inescapable misery. Becoming clear of their own mess and fully embracing that beautiful kid in their own hearts is just as hard for everyone else as it is for you. When they lash out at you, in most cases they are actually just fighting for their own breath of fresh air and you just happen to be in their line of fire. Accept in your heart that their mess is not about you, and have the courage and faith to lay their burdens at their feet. Don't hold on to their misery. Forgive them, and let it go.

- **Choose to forgive yourself**. Nothing in this world that is part of the pigsty is a part of what it means to be human. Becoming clear of your own mess and fully embracing that beautiful kid in your own heart is just as hard for you as it is for everyone else. Accept in your heart that all the mess you see is not really you. Don't hold on to the misery. Forgive yourself, and let it go.

- **Accept forgiveness**. Nothing in this world that is part of the pigsty is a part of what it means to be human. Nothing in this world that is part of the pigsty is a part of what it means to be you. Don't hold on to the misery. Forgive yourself, and let it go.

- **Choose to love**. Nothing in this world that is part of the pigsty is a part of what it means to be human. Nothing in this world that is part of the pigsty is a part of what it means to be you. Nothing in this world that is part of the pigsty is a part of what it means to be anyone else. Love everyone and everything made by God. Love everyone and everything of beauty co-created by people. God is everywhere and in all things. So, choose to love the Child of God in every human being. Love their shoes, love the walls, love the coffee mugs, love lazy afternoons, love sunshine, love rain. Choose to love all of creation – starting with yourself – from the inside out.

- **Choose not to hurt others**. Everyone you meet is a Child of God; every singe person you meet is made in His image and likeness.

God is everywhere and in all people. Every single time you choose to hurt someone, you are choosing to hurt part of His creation, and you are choosing to add a molten pile of slag to the world... you are choosing to bury yourself and anyone near you deeper into the pigsty. Choose not to pave that way.

- **Refuse to be hurt by others**. If you're living in a pigsty with people who enjoy being pigs, go find a river or a meadow. Nothing in this world that is part of the pigsty is a part of what it means to be human. There will always be some who enjoy being more like pigs than people. The problem is that it's only fun for them when they can get others to get stuck in the mud, too. It is hard to get out of the muck, but it is a lot easier to do when you are surrounded more by people focused on washing away their messes and shining from within than those who think digging you in deeper is a good thing.

- **Exorcism**. I don't mean the sensations you see in movies or on TV. I mean a rite that can affirm for the hidden nooks and crannies of your spirit that it is really just you and God inside... that all of this other stuff you see and feel is not really a part of you. I have no need or desire to debate the existence of forces fighting against you or the power of whatever has a grip on your heart or spirit. What matters is how real the struggles feel to you. A rite of exorcism can be a powerful and tangible reminder that anything truly inside you is a gift from God, that you exist to be loved and protected, that you deserve to fully understand what it means to be a Child of God. You are already perfect; no one and nothing can take that away from you.

- **Something uniquely you**. You are already perfect, and there is a part of you that knows the truth of what you need. It may be something that has worked for millions, and it may be something that will help only you. Find your truth, love your truth, and choose to live your truth. If your heart sings, you'll keep listening to the wisdom inside you.

10

Clearing the way — Routine pruning, or peeling a layer at a time

The Pevensie children of the original Narnia books spent an entire lifetime in Narnia before returning to our world as children. Growing up in Narnia, they all but forgot their former lives in England, which seemed like long lost dreams. But after falling back through the wardrobe into the lives they'd left behind, their memories as kings and queens of Narnia always felt a little more real than day-to-day life, like a gentle but constant calling in their hearts to find a way back home. Well... at least for three of the four children.

The child that God has created in each of us is much like those kings and queens of Narnia; when we are able to fully embrace the presence of God within us, the troubles of the "real" world can feel... small... distant... even disconnected. Just as seeing Aslan for the first time filled Lucy with an undying longing for more, the joy and simplicity of being what God has created creates its own insatiable desire to be closer to the divinity that loves and surrounds us.

But we have a choice. We can be like Susan and pretend the best of us is only a dream, choosing to be distracted and burdened by the world. Or, we can be like Lucy, who can see Aslan even when no one else can. What's the difference between the two? Lucy keeps looking.

Perhaps you have already made the choice to jump into faith with both feet and want to sluff off the muck and the mire so it doesn't build up; perhaps you are digging your way out of the darkness for the first time and are desperately looking for that first glimpse of light; perhaps you are somewhere in between.

Regardless, chipping away barriers smothering the kid in you and the life in your heart you know you deserve is much like Eustace Clarence Scrubb peeling away one layer of skin at a time. It's a slow process, but every layer you remove is one step closer to feeling lighter in your spirit.

The goal here is to fully embrace the kid in you and give it permission to embrace all of you. The goal here is to remember what it feels like to live in a world – even an imaginary world – where things just makes sense. The goal here is to be in the moment, surrounded by beauty, laughter, and a glorious sense of freedom... even if it is just one small moment at a time.

- **Read children's books**. Go to the local library and grab a handful of kids books at random. Or track down the books you loved to read when you were small. Don't just read them, get lost in them. Like a little kid, picture yourself inside the pages sniffing green eggs and ham. Put on a big yellow hat and look for ways to get into mischief. Fall asleep on a bed in a department store. Turn a flight of stairs into ice and slide down over and over on your belly. Hold on to an umbrella and let the wind take you for a flight. Remember what it feels like to see wonder and magic in everyone and everything.

- **Read scripture**. Or even better, read scriptures with lots of pictures that have been translated for younger readers. Imagine seeing miracles come to life all around you. Feel the peace and awe of a prophet personally teaching you about God. Imagine the voice of your favorite actor or narrator reading the stories to you and imagine you are in the stories. Experience the sense of infinite possibility that comes with sitting in and soaking up the glory and the goodness of the presence of God.

- **Wade or swim (safely) in living water.** Pools are great, but they don't offer the same experience as swimming in water that moves because of the power of the earth, the wind, the sun, and the moon. Brooks, streams, rivers, rainstorms, and oceans carry their own sense of life within them. The world around you has heaped refuse on you from every which way. Now, step into living water and feel the world wash away those troubles one wave or one splash at a time.

- **Roast hotdogs or marshmallows over a campfire.** Fire has a strength you can see, hear, and feel; when you cook things over a live fire, it has a power you can taste. Yes, you can cook things on the stove, in the oven, in a barbecue, or even in a kettle on the fire. But holding one end of the stick, slowly turning it so the food doesn't burn, and having to continually adjust how close you and the food are to the heart of the flame puts you in charge. It gives you control over the change in color and taste and texture. You co-create something that nourishes you. It is a tangible reminder that you can directly influence what happens in your life, which makes the food and your enjoyment of it even better.

- **Get lost in childhood songs, movies, and TV shows.** What did you watch or listen to over and over and over and over and over and over and over again? Why was it so fascinating to you? Step fully into that childlike wonder and experience it at least three more times. Don't watch or listen with a grown-up mind; don't analyze the experience. If it helps, invite friends over to share it with you. Sing and dance in your living room, shout the lines out loud, wear a sheet like a cape with your winter boots on.

- **Something uniquely you**. You are already perfect, and there is a part of you that already knows how to enjoy being a kid. Let it feel silly. Let it feel wonderful. Don't worry about being embarrassed – kids are too busy living to worry about what others see. Practice being a kid, and then practice being that kid in other parts of your day-to-day life. When you walk in the door to work, quietly imagine yourself skipping or karate kicking. When you answer the phone, picture a cartoon operator on the other end of the line. When you are pressed with a deadline, imagine you're a toy car racing to the finish line. When you are sitting down to a meal, imagine that you have eighteen hands all trying to shove food into your mouth at the same time. If people ask you why you are smiling, tell them the truth... maybe something like "I like to try and make small moments in life fun and surprising, so I pictured *blank*." (Try not to be surprised if they laugh with you or take a few minutes to join in the fun.) Simply do whatever it takes to practice being a kid in more parts of your life.

I I

Clearing the way
— Ongoing weeding as needed

Have you ever noticed that grass grows in the darndest places? It can peek up through concrete, tree roots, snow, sand, and more. Even if you put a thick layer of plastic under a mound of garden soil, grass will find a way to grow.

While it can be easy to be a kid sometimes, it can be just as easy to forget to try. Everyone around you – whether they mean to or not – is adding to the pigsty of the world around you; some of it's going to fall on you. Just like grass, it'll plant seeds that will poke through the landscape of happiness and freedom you are working so hard to cultivate. So, just like a gardener, the more you prune and weed the little things that get in your way, the fewer distractions you will encounter. But this work is hard; it takes practice, dedication, and persistence. So, don't start with the thing you "should" do that weighs a thousand pounds in your heart. Start by building a habit of something small and easy you'll love doing, and then work your way up to the types of weeding that feel like work. The more you prune, the better results you'll get – especially from those harder disciplines that feel like work.

Every little bit of weeding you do, in your head, your heart, your body, and your spirit, will help make other small weeds easier to remove, and larger obstacles easier to manage:

- **Consistently get enough sleep**. Have you ever noticed that a child has literally grown overnight? Well, the kid in you needs sleep, too. Yes, you need sleep to rest and to decompress, and to be able to take care of your responsibilities with a clear mind. But you also need sleep for your energy, imagination, and creativity to blossom and grow. And figure out when you get the best sleep. Maybe you sleep best from 9 pm to 5 am, or midnight to 8 am. Maybe a two-hour nap every Sunday afternoon will make your entire week better.

- **Learn to do something new** that requires your undivided attention at least once a week. Do something new that engages your mind and your body at the same time, but something that is different from how you normally spend your time. If you spend most of your day at a desk and in front of a computer, taking up gaming doesn't count. If you spend all day doing heavy lifting, taking up karate doesn't count. It needs to be something completely different. Be respectful of your physical limitations, but choose the courage to push yourself. A few possibilities: tai chi, knitting, swimming, pottery, fencing, guitar lessons, yoga, 65mprove theater, painting, long distance running, leather working, skeet shooting, gardening, voice lessons, canning, cosmetology, woodworking, writing a short story, archery, rowing, and drawing. It doesn't need to be larger than life, just something that lifts your mind and your body out of your normal routine.

- **Refuse to criticize anyone or anything**. Life is hard, so choose compassion over criticism. When you find yourself thinking or saying something negative or sarcastic, close your mouth and think at the other person, "Please forgive me for my thoughts against you, and please know that I wish you no harm. I love and appreciate that God is within you and all around you. Thank you for reminding me of my own humanity. Thank you for helping me remember to love and to be kinder to myself." If you can do so and it would not be inappropriate, lightly touch whomever you are addressing in order to help reconnect your own humanity with theirs. This can also work with objects that bring up negative emotions in you.

• **Establish and maintain a personal ritual of prayer, mindfulness, and/or meditation.** Don't buy into the hype over which form of stillness is "best" for you" Figure out what works for you. Maybe you need a mantra of sounds or words so your mind has a point of focus other than your internal chatter. Maybe you need to keep a gratitude journal. Maybe you need a moving qigong exercise to comfort and recharge your body and mind. The question is, what will help you find more internal peace? The only right answer is the one that helps you.

- **Embrace doubt, uncertainty, and mystery**. Say "I don't know" at least once a day. Say "you may be right" at least twice a day. Say "please" and "thank you" all the time. Eliminate words like "but" and "however" from your spoken vocabulary so that you stop making excuses. Learn to live with doubt and uncertainty. Doubt – like most things in the world – is not actually a part of you. It's a tool that creates and holds a space for something new or unexpected. If you have all the answers, you have nothing left to learn. You are one person on a planet of eight billion people speaking over 7,000 languages who have been learning for over 30,000 years. Even if you are the most intelligent and educated person in the entire world, remember that compared to all of the knowledge and experience of human history, what separates you from the six-year-old building a castle at the beach is roughly the size of a speck of sand. Instead of reminding yourself and everyone in your presence of how much you know, dedicate your time and energy to curiosity and mystery. The most amazing parts of your life may not have happened yet, and you don't want to miss them by being too full of yourself to notice.

- **Spirituality, worship, and religion.** It's probably an oversimplification, but I think of *spirituality* as the choice to believe in something much bigger than us, *worship* as actively celebrating what we believe in, and *religion* as the language consistently used to describe and explain what we choose to believe, the actions and behaviors that express what we believe, and the actions and behaviors that remind us of what we believe. For me, *faith* is the complete package: it is what I believe, my choice to believe, how I manifest my belief, and my relationship with all that I believe in. What reminds you that the universe is bigger than your own personal experience? Why do you believe you are more than a figment of someone's imagination? What do you do to remind yourself that what you believe and what you believe in matters?

How do you refocus when your doubt is bigger than your faith? What can you add to your life as a constant reminder that you are already perfect?

- **Go play outside**. Remind yourself of the beauty and vastness of God's creation by being part of it. Garden. Hike. Watch sunrises and sunsets. Build sandcastles. Dance in the rain. Walk barefoot through the mud. Climb a tree. Swing in a hammock. Drink from a hose. Swing from the monkey bars.

- **Something uniquely you**. If you are still alive today, there is something that a part of you has been living for. What makes your heart go pitter-patter? What makes your mouth water or your blood race? What makes you leap to your feet – literally or metaphorically – with excitement and anticipation? Live out loud because God is listening. Do whatever will help you end each and every day with this thought: "I am made in the image and likeness of God – how cool is that?!"

I 2

Being a grown-up kid
in a grown-up world

To be clear, in helping you fully embrace the kid in you I am not suggesting you neglect your very adult obligations. Quite the contrary. In the book of Ecclesiastes, there are two gifts from God: the people in our lives and the work that we do. Instead of avoiding our lives, I'm saying that believing God created you, knowing you are already perfect, and working to continually wash away the goop that builds up around you from this pigsty of a crazy world will help you live in a world filled with far more light. It will help you be more fully engaged in the life you have been given. It will help you live a life that creates light and invites healing for the people that you love.

The world would be a better place if everyone simply chose to be a decent human being. And I believe that any choice to the contrary is a personal choice, and that such a choice is never pleasing to God.

But I also believe that making better choices is just the beginning.

God created you. There is nothing in the universe that He loves more than you. At the end of the day, that's a pretty awesome place to start.

Epilogue

Thank you for spending this time with me. For reading. For listening.

I chose faith on my 28th birthday, and it was one of the most frightening and joy-filled moments of my life. In a lot of ways, it was also the beginning of things getter harder before they could get better.

This was in part because my spirit was buried under so much muck that it often felt like living under lava that had cooled to an impenetrable crust. It was in part because I didn't know how to be a person, let alone anyone in particular. It was because I had never learned about love.

I was very much a Eustace Clarence Scrubb who, despite all my clawing and scrabbling, could only scratch the surface of my spirit even when desperate to make a change.

For me, the choice to choose faith was about the leap of faith to believe there was a brink that I could not see in all the darkness, the choice of hope that within me was a glimmer of light, and the absolute commitment to hold onto that hope of a light with every fiber of my being, even when it felt like there was no light anywhere in the world.

I accepted on faith my two gifts: God as the primary person in my life, and the day-to-day work of choosing to believe that God created me. It took seven years for me to begin to see the light of God shining through me and through my life. It took seven years for me to open my heart enough to no longer feel alone. It took seven years before my heart believed what my brain had chosen to believe and what my spirit had known all along. And for a moment in time, I knew exactly what it meant to be whole.

On my 28th birthday I knew that I was choosing to choose faith, and I knew that I had a long Journey before me to try and find and live that faith. I did not know what my life would bring. I did not know who I would be. I did not know if life would get better. All I knew was that choosing to try to become what God created in me had to be far better than anything I had ever known or done.

Here is the part, though, for which I was fully unprepared. The more I cleared away the clutter and the distractions, the more I became who I already was. At first, each new revelation of what was really me was awful. I felt remorse, humiliation, anger, fear, resentment, and at times downright horror and disgust. It was not a fun process.

What I had to come to understand and accept about my choices is that I had made each choice for a reason. And if I was honest with myself, if faced with exactly the same situation today from that same foundation, I might very well make the same choices. My spiritual father at the time called it "a reasonable response to unreasonable circumstances."

The heart of the battle for me was believing that — in my core — there was nothing wrong with me. There was something horribly wrong with a lot of things that I had done and that had happened to me. But I had to learn and understand that there was nothing wrong with *me*.

I couldn't begin to chip away at the things wrong with my life and create better circumstances for myself until I faced myself honestly... until I made choices based on the foundation in me that was created by God and not on the foundation of muck created by the world around me... until I could truly see and accept myself first and foremost as a Child of God.

This for me really was the beginning. And if any of my descriptions of living in this pigsty of our world resonate within you, my hope for you is that you will find your own beginning. God exists outside of space and time. That means your beginning is His beginning. And no matter what you think, say, or do, God has the first and the final word about the little kid – the core – in you.

He created you, and God doesn't make mistakes. You are a part of all that is holy and all that is good. You are beautiful. You are loved. You are already perfect.

You are a Child of God.

Acknowledgements

To my oldest and dearest friends... *Thank you for giving me, in love, the space I needed to learn how to be me.*

David Griffiths
Elizabeth Sahady
Genevieve Worley Brown
Larry & Stella Hoy
Linda Michele Ballinger
Michael Hora
Sarah Allen Dutkevitch
Stephen Smith

To Chaplain Bruce Mentzer, Father Peter Smith, Father Joseph (Morris), Father Don Hock, Khouria Maggie Hock... *Thank you for refusing to let me be less than I am created to be.*

To Chaplain Mark Sahady... *Thank you for the gift of unconditional love, acceptance, forgiveness, and faith. You saw the Child of God in me long before I knew it was there to be seen. I am, in many ways, the person I am today because you chose faith in me. With all my love, thank you.*

Acknowledgments regarding this book project... Beta readers, thank you for helping me believe in this book: Suzan David, Megan Wolf, Maghan Moslander-Fleming, Arika Davis, and Amy Halstead

Editor and incredibly forgiving partner: David N. Griffiths. Faith and support: The three coolest kids in the world

Photographer Larry Kanfer
Cover art Top Book Designer
Cover design Isak Griffiths
Book formatting done in Vellum
DIY process learned primarily from Joanna Penn
DIY technique learned primarily from Joseph Michael

Thank you all!

My Reading List

There is no bibliography because the "research" for this book has been my own life. Instead of a list of academic resources, here is a list of topics I routinely use to refresh my spirit, stay motivated, and believe in miracles.

Reconnecting with the kid in me

- All things hobbits
- All things Narnia
- All things Star Trek
- All things Seuss
- All things Julie Andrews
- Curious George
- Paddington Bear
- Mr. Popper's Penguins

Restoring my faith in humanity

- *People will Talk* (1951), with Carry Grant and Jeanne Crain
- *While You Were Sleeping* (1995), with

Sandra Bullock and Bill Pullman
- *The Hobbit* (1977), created by Rankin/Bass
- Books by Honor Raconteur
- *Ender* books by Orson Scott Card

Believing anything is possible

- *The Book of Akathists*, by Holy Trinity Monastery
- *Love Wins: A Book about Heaven, Hell, and the Fate of Every Person Who Ever Lived*, by Rob Bell
- *You Can Heal Your Life (unabridged, adapted for audio)*, by Louise L. Hay
- *Light Warrior: Connecting with the Spiritual Power of Fierce Love*, by Kyle Gray
- *Becoming Magic: A Course in Manifesting an Exceptional Life*, by Genevieve Davis

Reminding myself that change really is incredibly hard – and worth it

- *Blink: The Power of Thinking Without Thinking*, by Malcolm Gladwell

- *Star Trek: Discovery: The Way to the Stars*, by Una McCormack
- *Pre-Suasion: Channeling Attention for Change*, by Robert Cialdini Ph.D.
- *Imager* books by L.E. Modesitt Jr.

Staying motivating while writing and publishing my first book

- *How to Make a Living with Your Writing: Books, Blogging and More*, by Joanna Penn
- *Money Loves You: Easy Manifestation Secrets Revealed*, by Blair Robertson
- *Write. Publish. Repeat.: The No-Luck Guide to Self-Publishing Success*, by Johnny B. Truant, Sean Platt

About the Author

Isak Griffiths is an indie-authorpreneur, inspirational speaker, artist, musician, and Orthodox Christian. She's originally from the south side of Chicago, an Air Force veteran, a former database programmer, a seasoned manager and executive, and an Illinois MBA. "Isak" is a form of Isaac, which means "laughing" and is pronounced "ee-SOCK."

When she was 23, she found herself without a job, without a home, without a degree, and without a plan; so, she put her stuff in storage, moved to Hawaii, and became a beach bum. There has always been a part of her that believes that when we feel broken, we can act to make things better. But it took her a long time to figure out how to make better choices on purpose instead of as a reaction to fear and pain. Now she has a passion for helping others see how extraordinary they are, how much they are loved, and how often miracles happen when we simply get out of the way.

If you appreciated this book, she would appreciate your letting others know about her work:

- write a book review on your favorite book platform,
- ask your local library to carry the book,
- post a testimonial on honestimpact.com,
- invite her to deliver your group's key note address,
- give a gift in her name to her favorite nonprofits (Holy Apostles in Bloomington, Illinois, Courage Connection in Champaign, Illinois, and the YWCA of UIUC) in Champaign, Illinois, and/or
- tell your friends.

To learn more about the work she is doing to help people embrace the kid deep down inside and get out from under the muck that has been piled on them in this crazy, mixed-up world — go to honestimpact.com.

About the Text

Child of God was written with the audio version in mind. Therefore it it very much written in my voice – the way I would say it out loud. In fact, the final revision of the text was done by recording the audio version and then editing the text to match.

The non-standard punctuation in the text is done to help facilitate hearing the words as you read. For example, because the primary meaning of a thought can shift depending on which word is stressed, the use of italics within a sentence highlights the meaning suggested by stressing *that* particular word over the meaning suggested by *stressing* that particular word.

If there is a comma missing where you might expect one on a page it's because I wouldn't actually pause there when saying the words out loud, and adding a comma isn't needed for the meaning to be clear. You'll find that I always use the Oxford comma because I want you to know that I love my friends, my life, my kids, Harvey the Pooka, and Katherine

Hepburn; I don't want to risk you thinking that I love my kids, Harvey the Pooka and Katherine Hepburn.

Semicolons between sentences represent a single thought that requires a second sentence to be clear; when spoken, semicolons sound like a sentence that didn't begin with a capital letter and that somehow still makes total sense.

Sometimes I end thoughts, sentences, or even paragraphs with an ellipsis. That's because I'm asking you to do two things at the same time: 1) sit with that last thought for a moment before going on, and 2)...

Understand that ellipses usually represent... a natural pause within a single thought... or perhaps a change of focus within that thought. Text that is repeated verbatim or with subtle changes reflect the fact that – when spoken – repetition is a gentle but powerful emphasis.

Text that is repeated verbatim or with subtle changes are intended to be heard using different tones, different pacing, and different volumes. Text that is repeated verbatim or with subtle changes are done because the point being made really matters.

Good luck. And when stuck, read the words out loud... pretend that I'm reading them to you myself, or that you are reading them to a friend who needs the words more than you.

To All of You

... Especially the Reader

Thank you!

The End

Notes & Thoughts

Notes & Thoughts